DATE DUE

GAYLORD   PRINTED IN U.S.A.

ANDREW CARNEGIE

CAPTAIN OF INDUSTRY

SPECIAL LIVES IN HISTORY THAT BECOME

ANDREW
CARNEGIE
CAPTAIN OF INDUSTRY

by Dana Meachen Rau

Content Adviser: Jeremy Atack, Ph.D.,
Professor, Departments of Economics and History,
Vanderbilt University

Reading Adviser: Rosemary G. Palmer, Ph.D.,
Department of Literacy, College of Education,
Boise State University

COMPASS POINT BOOKS MINNEAPOLIS, MINNESOTA

Compass Point Books
3109 West 50th Street, #115
Minneapolis, MN 55410

Visit Compass Point Books on the Internet at *www.compasspointbooks.com*
or e-mail your request to *custserv@compasspointbooks.com*

For Vita, my favorite librarian, who shares the light that books hold.

Editor: Jennifer VanVoorst
Lead Designer: Jaime Martens
Photo Researcher: Marcie C. Spence
Page Production: Heather Griffin
Cartographer: XNR Productions, Inc.
Educational Consultant: Diane Smolinski

Managing Editor: Catherine Neitge
Creative Director: Keith Griffin
Editorial Director: Carol Jones

Library of Congress Cataloging-in-Publication Data
Rau, Dana Meachen, 1971–
  Andrew Carnegie: captain of industry / by Dana Meachen Rau.
    p. cm. — (Signature lives)
  Includes bibliographical references and index.
  ISBN 0-7565-0995-5
  1. Carnegie, Andrew, 1835–1919—Juvenile literature. 2.
Industrialists—United States—Biography—Juvenile literature. 3.
Philanthropists—United States—Biography—Juvenile literature. I. Title.
II. Series.
CT275.C3R388 2006
  338.7′672′092—dc22   2005002680

Signature Lives

MODERN AMERICA

Starting in the late 19th century, advancements in all areas of human activity transformed an old world into a new and modern place. Inventions prompted rapid shifts in lifestyle, and scientific discoveries began to alter the way humanity viewed itself. Beginning with World War I, warfare took place on a global scale, and ideas such as nationalism and communism showed that countries were taking a larger view of their place in the world. The combination of all these changes continues to produce what we know as the modern world.

Table of Contents

1 LET THERE BE LIGHT

Chapter

❦⟨∽⟩❧

Andrew Carnegie didn't expect such excitement at his arrival in Dunfermline, Scotland. Carnegie, his mother, and some close friends rode on a horse-drawn coach that he had built for this seven-week trip through Britain's countryside. Now, on July 27, 1881, he was returning to the small village in Scotland where he was born 46 years earlier.

Carnegie was eager to see the friends and sites he missed, but he had a different reason for his visit. He was there to dedicate the building of a free public library, for which he was providing the funds. Carnegie believed books were vital to success. He hoped that a library would be a window to the world that the people of Dunfermline might not have had access to before.

An early 20th-century cartoon shows Andrew Carnegie, builder of libraries. Carnegie used his vast wealth to provide libraries so that knowledge could be available to all.

When his coach entered Dunfermline, Carnegie could not believe his eyes. The village had declared the day a holiday in honor of its native son. Flags, banners, and flowers covered the buildings, and a brass band and Scottish bagpipes filled the air with music. Hundreds of people clapped and waved as the town officials welcomed Carnegie and his traveling party. He was so overcome with emotion that he cried.

Carnegie had first left Scotland for the United States more than 30 years before. His family had been penniless. The United States offered them the hope of a better life. During his visits back to Scotland, including this one, Carnegie felt his hometown looked much smaller than he remembered. Perhaps it was because he was just a child when he left. Or perhaps it was because he had grown—not just in size and age, but in many other ways as well.

The highest aspiration Carnegie had as a child was to become a weaver like his father. But in the United States, he had been successful in a number of fields and ultimately became the leader of a booming new industry—the manufacture of steel. Even with his great success in America, Carnegie was immensely proud of his Scottish roots. "It's a God's mercy I was born a Scotchman," he wrote in his travel diary, "for I do not see how I could ever have been contented to be anything else."

Carnegie was pleased with all the money he had made. He had earned it by hard work and smart choices. But he had so much money that he wanted to give some away. It was his responsibility, he believed, to distribute wealth to the community.

The Carnegie Library in Dunfermline was the first of many he would provide the money to build. Carnegie was pleased to give his mother, Margaret, the honor of laying the foundation stone of this first library with a special silver trowel made just for the occasion. Over the entrance to the library, Carnegie recommended that the architect carve the phrase

The library in Riverside, California, is one of many Carnegie donated in his lifetime.

Andrew Carnegie felt a responsibility to share his wealth with others.

"Let There Be Light" with the image of a rising sun. This sunlight, of course, represented the knowledge the books would bring. In his lifetime, Carnegie donated millions of dollars to build thousands of libraries all over the world, and many of the libraries greet patrons with these same inspiring words.

Though Carnegie received little formal education, he spent a lifetime educating himself through books and experiences. His great achievements in many industries led to great wealth. Carnegie's life is an example of the American dream. Through his gifts of libraries and other institutions, he gave back to his adopted country the gift it gave him: the hope of knowledge and the chance for success. ℘

Beginning with the library in Dunfermline, Scotland, Andrew Carnegie donated funds to build 2,811 libraries in the United States and throughout the world. During his lifetime, he gave away $350 million of his great fortune to build public libraries, establish educational institutions, and fund peace initiatives.

Chapter
2 A WEAVER'S SON

eↄ⌒ⱺↄ

*D*unfermline is nestled in the hills of Scotland north-west of Edinburgh. In ancient times, it had been the capital of Scotland. The remains of a large stone abbey and the palace of Robert the Bruce, Scotland's first king, are as much a part of the landscape as the flower-covered glen.

Carnegie felt lucky to have been born there. "The child privileged to develop amid such sur-roundings," he once wrote, "absorbs poetry and romance with the air he breathes, assimilates history and tradition as he gazes around." On the cobblestone corner of Moodie Street and Priory Lane stood a small cottage. Andrew Carnegie was born on November 25, 1835, in the large room of its second floor. It was this day that he first heard the

When Carnegie was young, weavers like his father worked at home, weaving cloth by hand on large looms.

bells of the abbey, which sounded daily throughout his youth. From his beginnings, Carnegie was reminded of the importance of his little town in Scotland's history.

Dunfermline was a town of weavers. These craftsmen worked out of their homes, weaving linen cloth by hand on their looms. Almost half the population of Dunfermline was weavers. The designs on tablecloths and linens they produced were as fine as tapestries, and their products fetched a high price.

Dunfermline Abbey is the burial site of many Scottish kings and queens.

Andrew's father, William Carnegie, was one of these weavers. During the day, William worked on his large looms set up on the first floor of the

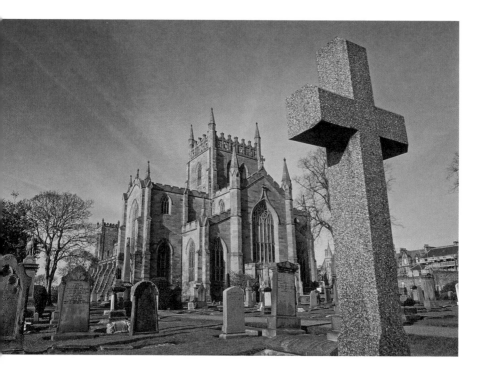

cottage. Each evening, he retired upstairs with little Andra (his name for Andrew) and his wife, Margaret, where they ate and slept. William was well respected for his ability to weave cloth. His operation was so large that he even employed four assistants. Only a year after Andrew was born, William bought more looms and moved his family up the road to a larger house on Edgar Street.

> The town of Dunfermline was the center in Scotland for weaving damask linen, a sturdy white material used to make napkins and tablecloths. Andrew's father owned several of the nearly 3,500 looms in town.

The weaving of cloth filled the house with a constant rhythm of the clicking looms. Andrew liked to watch his father, dressed in a clean, white apron, weave as he threaded the shuttle left to right, while pushing his feet on the pedals with dexterity. Andrew assumed that he, too, would be a weaver when he grew up. He idolized his father and his trade.

While his family lived a simple existence, learning new things was always important to them. The weavers almost always took a break for an hour around noontime, when they met out in the streets for a smoke, a chat, or to read the newspaper. They often had lively religious and political discussions. Andrew was not old enough to be involved in their talks, but he discovered the power of discussion and

Andrew Carnegie was born in this cottage in Dunfermline, Scotland.

learning even at his young age.

Like many other children in Dunfermline, however, Andrew did not start school right away. Unlike today, there were no laws that said children had to attend school. Many children needed to work to help their families survive. William and Margaret Carnegie had decided Andrew did not have to start school until he asked. But as he grew older, they were afraid he was never going to ask. When Andrew was 8, they called the schoolmaster of the

Rolland School, Mr. Martin, and asked him to invite Andrew on their next outing. Carnegie later wrote:

> *He took me upon an excursion one day with some of my companions who attended school, and great relief was experienced by my parents when one day soon afterward I came and asked for permission to go to Mr. Martin's school.*

Andrew loved school from his first day. The Rolland School was only a one-room schoolhouse that was very cold and heated by a fire in winter. Still, to Andrew, "The school was a perfect delight to me and if anything occurred which prevented my attendance I was unhappy." It greatly upset him that he was often late. When he needed to fetch water for his mother from the town well in the morning, older women often chatted in line holding him up.

Outside school, Andrew spent his time with his Uncle Lauder and his cousin George. Uncle Lauder owned a shop on High Street where he sold fresh fruit and vegetables. When Uncle

Andrew loved to keep pets. He started with pigeons. Then his yard housed more than a dozen rabbits in cages built for him by his father. Saturdays, his day off from school, he spent gathering dandelions and clover for the rabbits to eat. He organized his friends, letting them call a rabbit their own, so that they would help collect food for them as well.

Lauder wasn't busy with customers, he was teaching Andrew and George about Scottish heroes, such as the brave William Wallace or Robert the Bruce. He taught them history and to be proud of Scotland. He read the boys poems and plays which he then had them memorize and recite. Andrew called George "Dod" and George called him "Naig." Together they acted out the plays, especially the battle scenes.

These talks of history and its heroes inspired Andrew. Even when deciding which route to take home—the dark route through the eerie churchyard of the abbey, or the lit streets through the May Gate, Andrew always chose the abbey. He thought of William Wallace and was brave.

Around this time, in 1843, Andrew's little brother Thomas was born. The family was growing. But there would be sadness soon to come. A textile mill opened in Dunfermline. It held 20 looms that ran by steam power. Steam engines ran machines that could work more quickly and more cheaply than people ever could.

More cloth was made by the mill, and less by the handloom

The Industrial Revolution brought with it the steam engine, which could power looms that wove cloth in a factory setting. Before this, weavers picked up their yarn from a merchant and then brought it back to their homes to weave on their own looms. Because the weavers worked in their own cottages, this type of work was called a cottage industry.

weavers of the town, including William Carnegie. Even though William's cloth was better made, customers bought the mill-made cloth. It was cheaper, and they could get it sooner.

Textile mills mass-produced cloth that once was woven by hand.

The Carnegie family suffered. William had to sell off some of his looms, and the family moved back to a smaller house on Moodie Street. Margaret took on the challenge of supporting her family. Tending to the cooking, cleaning, and her boys and husband were a large enough job. But to make money for the family, she opened a shop at the house and sold vegetables and candy. She also found work with William's brother, who was a shoemaker. Even Andrew helped out keeping the books. "I became useful to my parents even at the early age of ten," he wrote.

William could find no work, and Margaret's jobs did not bring in enough money to support them. They were very poor and something had to be done. A few years before, two of Margaret's sisters and a brother-in-law had left for America and settled in Pittsburgh. They assured Margaret in their letters that her family would be able to find work there.

The Carnegies wanted the best for their two blond-haired, blue-eyed boys, Andrew, now 12, and Tom, now 5. They sold the remaining looms, as well as all of their furniture, at an auction. But they did not have enough money to book passage on a ship to America. They had to borrow money from a family friend and baker, Ella Ferguson, who lived up the street. They promised to repay her when they could. Soon

Andrew's Uncle Lauder was almost as enthusiastic about the United States as he was about Scotland. He respected the Founding Fathers for throwing off the oppression of English rule. He kept an album with pictures of those figures he admired, including Benjamin Franklin, George Washington, Thomas Jefferson, and others. Lauder's strong feelings about the new nation made the Carnegies optimistic about their new life in the United States.

they were ready to go.

In the evenings, William sang to his boys in anticipation:

To the West, to the West,
  to the land of the free,
Where the mighty Missouri
  rolls down to the sea;
Where a man is a man
  even though he must toil
And the poorest may gather
  the fruits of the soil.

The Carnegies were hopeful. In 1848, they set off for the United States of America. ❧

3 A NEW HOME

Chapter

❧⚬❧

Andrew was not eager to leave his home in Scotland and move to Pittsburgh. "I remember that I stood with tearful eyes looking out of the window until Dunfermline vanished from view," he later wrote, "the last structure to fade being the grand and sacred old Abbey." He cried as Uncle Lauder waved goodbye when they drove away.

The Carnegies set sail in May 1848 on the sailing ship the *Wiscassett*. Steamships were faster, but they were also more expensive, and the Carnegies could not afford steamship passage. A sailing ship held cargo and only a few passengers, and the journey was longer. The Carnegies' voyage across the Atlantic took seven weeks. They shared the ship with others hoping for a new life in America. In fact,

Andrew Carnegie was a young man when he came to the United States with his family.

in 1848, more people from Britain left for the United States than had ever before.

Once on the ship, Andrew's sadness ended and his excitement grew. While other passengers despised the rolling motion of the ship and the cramped bunks below deck, Andrew loved the adventure. He became friends with the sailors, relaying messages around the ship for them. He was even invited to dine with the sailors one evening.

Their arrival in New York Harbor was overwhelming. The harbor was crowded with immigrants like them, looking for their luggage, gathering their families, and deciding what to do next. While his father bought passage on a steamboat that would take them up the Hudson River, Andrew explored. One of the sailors he had befriended on the ship, Robert Barryman, bought Andrew a glass of sarsaparilla. An old woman served it to them from a fancy fountain. The bubbly, sweet, brown soda was a tasty welcome to this new country.

After the steamboat ride, they decided to travel by canal. Trains were not always reliable, nor

New York Harbor in the mid-1800s was a busy place. Immigrants from many countries, mostly in Europe, came to settle in America. Some came to avoid famines in their own countries. Others came looking for new job opportunities in the cities. In 1848, the year Carnegie and his family sailed from Scotland, 188,233 people came from Britain to America, more than ever had before.

were they safe. They boarded a canal boat that took them along the Erie Canal—a man-made waterway that crossed New York, connecting Albany to Lake Erie.

From the view on the canal boat, America seemed huge to Andrew. Passengers sat on the top of the boat and watched the countryside. The boat moved very slowly because it ran on horsepower. Along the canal's bank was a path, called a towpath, where a boy led or rode a horse that pulled the boat. Andrew liked to hop off the boat to the canal bank, make friends with the horse boys, and hop back again.

After a steamboat ride on the Ohio River, they

In Carnegie's time, immigrants to the United States were processed at New York's Castle Garden Immigration Station.

27

finally reached their destination—Pittsburgh, Pennsylvania. It had been a long and tiring journey. They were thrilled to see their family waiting for them. Aunt Aitken and Aunt and Uncle Hogan brought them to their home on Rebecca Street in Allegheny, right outside the city. Their town was a series of rough, wooden houses lining a muddy riverbank. Other working-class people, like themselves, lived in the town.

Carnegie's trip from Scotland to Pittsburgh was mostly by water.

Their house had a small weaver's shop out back. Andrew's aunts and uncle invited the Carnegies to live there. The Carnegies were glad to accept. They did not have the money to buy a house of their own. They would be able to make their home on the upper floor of the workshop. The bottom floor held a weaver's loom.

William Carnegie was overjoyed. He would be able to weave again. He was sure that people in America would be willing to pay a high price for his fine linen. Working hard all day, he wove checkered tablecloths and tried to sell them door-to-door. But no one was willing to buy. He soon found that, just as in Dunfermline, cheaper cloth was being produced by machines.

They had to make money somehow. Right away, Margaret went to Henry Phipps, the local cobbler on Rebecca Street, and offered her services as a shoemaker. He was able to give her a lot of work, which she could do at home.

His parents' hard work and hopefulness were traits Andrew admired in them. Even as a child, he knew this experience of being poor was building his character. He later wrote:

> *This is where the children of honest poverty have the most precious of advantages over those of wealth. ... The mother,*

*nurse, cook, governess, teacher, saint, all
in one; the father, exemplar, guide, coun-
selor, and friend! Thus were my brother
and I brought up. What has the child
of millionaire or nobleman that counts
compared to such a heritage?*

His mother's shoemaking was not enough to
support the family. There was no question—Andrew
and his father needed to find work, too. While
Andrew would much rather attend school like his
younger brother, he knew it was important to bring
money into the family.

Both William and Andrew found jobs at the
Blackstock Cotton Mill, a cotton-weaving factory.
Andrew's first paying job earned him $1.20 a week.
"I have made millions since," Carnegie wrote later
in life, "but none of those millions gave me such
happiness as my first week's earnings." This money
came at a price. He and his father had to work long
hours. Though Andrew was barely a teenager, there
were no laws at that time that restricted the number
of hours a child could work. Even in the cold of
winter, he woke in the darkness to reach work by
6 A.M. At the end of the day, he left the factory at
6 P.M. and walked home in darkness as well. He only
had one day off a week.

Andrew's father was in charge of tending the
mill's large steam-powered looms. Andrew worked

as a bobbin boy, in charge of the machine that wound the thread around the large spools. These bobbins were then used by the weavers in another part of the factory. Andrew had to watch the bobbins closely. As soon as they were full of thread he had to replace them as fast as he could.

Bobbin boys stood on the spinning machine to replace full bobbins with empty ones.

Soon, Andrew was given a more important position, which earned him $2 a week. He tended the steam engine in the basement of the factory that ran the machines. Even though he was earning more money and had been given more responsibility, Andrew hated the job. The steam engine was like a monster, its boiler constantly needing feeding. If its temperature was too high, the boiler could explode. If its temperature was too low, the machines on the factory floor would stop working. Nightmares filled Andrew's sleep as he worried about keeping the boiler in perfect balance.

Thankfully, John Hay, his employer, needed him in his office. Andrew had good writing skills that Hay could put to use. He wanted a boy to help him write letters and do the bookkeeping. Andrew was even allowed to attend night classes to learn about double-entry bookkeeping, a new method that would improve Hay's business.

Being a clerk in the office was not his only job in the factory, however. He spent part of the day in the sunny office, but the rest of the day he was given the task of dipping threaded bobbins in vats of oil. The oil stuck to his skin and smelled horrid. He often was sick from the stench and imagined that even the brave Scottish heroes whom he admired—William Wallace and Robert the Bruce—would not be able to handle it either. For a boy who was often

Robert the Bruce, one of Carnegie's heroes, was a 14th-Century Scottish king; he is buried in Dunfermline Abbey.

optimistic, he wrote, "No bird that ever was confined in cage longed for freedom more than I." That freedom was soon to come. ✑

4 THROUGH THE STREETS AND ACROSS THE WIRES

❧❧❧

Andrew Carnegie felt he got his real start in life in 1850. That was the year Uncle Hogan came home one evening with exciting news of a new job. David Brooks, who ran the O'Reilly Telegraph Company, was looking for another messenger boy.

Carnegie couldn't wait to rush to Brooks for an interview. He would be making 50 cents more a week than at the textile mill. More importantly, however, he would see the city and its people each day instead of standing over smelly and repulsive vats of oil.

At first, Carnegie's father refused. He thought Andrew was too small. Such a scrawny, little boy would never be given such an active job of running through the streets of Pittsburgh to deliver mes-

Telegraph operators sent, received, and copied messages transmitted over the wires.

sages to important businessmen. But he finally agreed. Carnegie dressed in his best clothes, impressed Brooks in the interview, got the job, and began right away.

Carnegie was thrilled and saw this job as a first step on his road toward success. After his drudgery in the dark cellar,

> *I was lifted into paradise, yes, heaven, as it seemed to me, with newspapers, pens, pencils, and sunshine about me. There was scarcely a minute in which I could not learn something or find out how much there was to learn and how little I knew. I felt that my foot was upon the ladder and that I was bound to climb.*

The telegraph was a relatively new form of communication in America. Invented by Samuel Morse in 1837, the telegraph was based on sending electric pulses over wires. About 13 years later, when Carnegie began work as a messenger boy, telegraphy had become an important method of immediate communication.

The telegraph consisted of a long piece of paper tape spooled onto a wheel. This paper unwound under an arm, called a tapper key, that tapped a series of dots and dashes onto it. These dots and dashes represented letters and was called Morse code, after the inventor. A translator read the dots and dashes on the tape, typed up the message, and then handed it off to a messenger boy who delivered it to the intended receiver.

Pittsburgh was a hub of telegraph activity. The

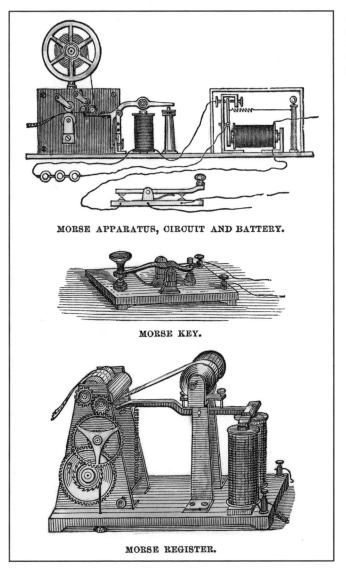

Morse's telegraph machine was made up of three primary parts.

MORSE APPARATUS, CIRCUIT AND BATTERY.

MORSE KEY.

MORSE REGISTER.

city was growing and becoming the center of business because of its position on the river where many goods were sent and received. Urgent and important messages often came into the office, and the boys had to deliver them to the businessmen of the city.

The messenger boys were a tight-knit group. Carnegie made friends in this bunch that he had for the rest of his life. They were an official-looking crew, dressed in uniforms of green jackets and short

Though Carnegie delivered messages on foot, messengers later in the century would use bicycles.

pants called knickerbockers.

At first overwhelmed by all the streets and addresses, Carnegie soon had them memorized. He excelled at his job, and was known for his speed at delivering messages. He was even paid more than the other boys because he was so fast. But the hours were long and the work was tiring. Carnegie started work at 7 A.M., and a few nights a week he had to stay until 11 P.M. He looked forward to the friendly folks during his travels. Sometimes the grocer slipped him some fruit, the baker shared a pastry, or the confectioner treated him to candy.

> *Early in his working life, Carnegie showed his ability to manage money and people. Telegrams delivered outside the city limits earned messengers an extra 10 cents. Carnegie set up a plan in which messengers deposited their extra earnings into a fund that was then divided equally among them at the end of the week.*

Carnegie especially liked to deliver messages to Mr. Foster at the Pittsburgh Theater. If he arrived with a message close enough to showtime, Foster always let Carnegie, and the other messenger boys, take the empty seats in the upstairs gallery. At the Pittsburgh Theater, Carnegie saw many Shakespearean plays. He memorized them, just as he had memorized poems with Uncle Lauder back in Dunfermline.

Carnegie and the other messenger boys found even more ways to exercise their minds. Together,

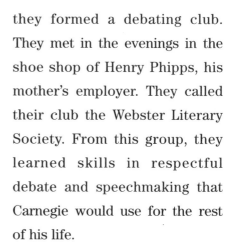

Colonel James Anderson donated his library to the city. Borrowers were charged $2 a year to use the library. Carnegie wrote letters to the city protesting that the charges were unfair to many working people of the time. The library eventually dropped the charges.

they formed a debating club. They met in the evenings in the shoe shop of Henry Phipps, his mother's employer. They called their club the Webster Literary Society. From this group, they learned skills in respectful debate and speechmaking that Carnegie would use for the rest of his life.

Books were not something Carnegie's family could afford. Nor were there libraries to provide them. Colonel James Anderson, a retired businessman in Pittsburgh, opened up a whole new world of knowledge for Carnegie. Anderson was very wealthy and had a personal collection of more than 400 books. He felt it was important to share them with working boys who might not otherwise have access to them. On Saturday evenings, the boys were invited to visit his home and borrow a book. If they returned it the next week, they could borrow another.

This experience was life-changing for Carnegie. He said:

The windows were opened in the walls of my dungeon through which the light of

*knowledge streamed in. Every day's toil
and even the long hours of night service
were lightened by the book which I carried
about with me and read in the intervals
that could be snatched from duty.*

From Anderson's generosity grew Carnegie's
love of libraries, which would play an important role
later in his life.

*Colonel James
Anderson had
a major
influence on
Carnegie's life.*

Back at the telegraph office, Carnegie was occasionally asked to watch the office while the manager was away. Carnegie couldn't help but listen to the clicking sound of the telegraph. He had heard of some telegraph operators who could translate messages just by listening to the clicks of the tapper key. Carnegie was soon able to write down the messages as they were received. Not many people could translate by ear in this way. At the time, Carnegie was said to be one of only three telegraph

Many messages were sent and received from this New York City telegraph office.

operators in the United States who could take messages without looking at the written dots and dashes. Carnegie's ability saved the telegraph office lots of time. People even visited the office to see this wonder boy. They couldn't believe that what he did could be done.

Soon, important businessmen asked Carnegie to send their messages because they thought he was the best man for the task. Carnegie was promoted to the job of telegraph operator. He was only 17 and already making $25 a month. It had only taken a year and a half to climb the ladder from messenger boy to telegraph operator. The Carnegie family was pleased. They were able to buy Uncle Hogan's house (he and the aunts had moved), and they could even pay back Ella Ferguson the money she lent them for their passage to the United States two years before. ✍

Chapter
5 RIDING THE RAILS

❧❧❧

Thomas Scott was one of the businessmen who came into the telegraph office and asked specifically for Carnegie to send his messages. To Carnegie, Scott embodied all that he hoped to be one day. Scott was the superintendent of the Pittsburgh division of the Pennsylvania Railroad, one of the largest businesses in the country at the time. He was successful and part of a business that was growing as America grew. Scott took a liking to Carnegie, too. He saw firsthand how quick Carnegie could learn and how clever he was.

In 1853, Scott asked Carnegie to join him. He needed a telegrapher and assistant in the office. The pay was higher than Carnegie was getting at the time, and his hours would be shorter. At the

Carnegie began work with the railroad at an exciting time, when a rail line across Pennsylvania was just beginning operation.

Pennsylvania Railroad office he would witness a good share of excitement. In 1852, just one year earlier, the railway line crossing Pennsylvania from Philadelphia to Pittsburgh had opened. Now Pittsburgh was connected to the East Coast by rail, instead of just by canal and river, so it was easier to trade and transport goods.

This rail line, however, was just a single set of tracks for both trains. Eastbound and westbound trains shared the same line. This led to numerous accidents. Trains might be on the tracks at the same time and collide with each other. Another problem was the condition of the tracks. The tracks were made of cast-iron rails laid on wood ties. The cast iron, especially in sudden cold weather, cracked and curled up, creating a huge danger to the trains and their passengers.

Scott was in charge of handling the trains on these tracks. With the telegraph, stations were better able to communicate with each other. Scott planned on having Carnegie send the telegraphs to control the movement of the trains. Soon, Carnegie became invaluable in the office. He became known as "Mr. Scott's Andy."

Another part of Carnegie's job was to visit the camps where men were laying new track or fixing those in need of repair. Until then, Carnegie had been used to the more refined men in the office. The freight conductors, brakemen, and others were a rough lot. But Andrew liked them and learned to work well with all types of people.

In the telegraph office, Scott was in charge of giving the orders, and Carnegie was in charge of sending them over the telegraph. One morning, however, Scott was not yet in, and there was a major problem. There had been an accident, and the people on the scene were not sure what to do. All of the trains were held up. Carnegie was torn. Should

Carnegie got to know many different kinds of railroad employees, including those who worked as brakemen.

he try to solve the problem, or should he wait for Scott to return. He decided something had to be done to prevent even more delays. Carnegie sent orders over the telegraph and cleared up the track. Scott was surprised Carnegie had been so bold. But he was impressed, too. He knew that Carnegie was going to make a good railway man.

Even though Carnegie was an excellent worker, he still made mistakes. On one such occasion, Scott sent him to Altoona, Pennsylvania, with the important task of picking up the packet of monthly paychecks for the employees of the railroad. He tucked the packet under his coat and boarded the train. Hanging on the outside of the train, Carnegie became fascinated watching how the train worked and chatting with its crew. Suddenly, Carnegie felt inside his jacket. The package was gone. Losing all of those valuable checks would surely mean the end of his job. He begged the conductor to go back. Searching frantically from the train, Carnegie saw the bundle tucked on the edge of a riverbank, just inches from falling into the river. From that day on, Carnegie decided to never be too rough on his employees, knowing that everyone makes mistakes sometimes.

In 1855, Carnegie's father died, and Carnegie was left to support his mother and brother, Tom. His father had tried to hold on to his tradition of weaving and never found the future he hoped for in the United States. Carnegie, on the other hand, was always looking for ways to grow with the country, securing his future as a successful businessman.

In addition to his income from the railroad office, Carnegie made extra money for his family by investing. He put money into companies he believed would do well. When they were successful, he was paid part of the profit. In 1856, on Scott's suggestion, Carnegie invested $500, which his mother borrowed from her brother, in the Adams Express Company. It was a smart investment. Every month, Carnegie received a check to help support

Because of their growing importance in the United States, railroads were a smart investment choice.

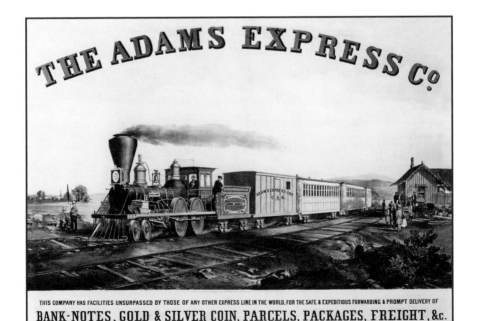

THE ADAMS EXPRESS Co

THIS COMPANY HAS FACILITIES UNSURPASSED BY THOSE OF ANY OTHER EXPRESS LINE IN THE WORLD, FOR THE SAFE & EXPEDITIOUS FORWARDING & PROMPT DELIVERY OF

BANK-NOTES, GOLD & SILVER COIN, PARCELS, PACKAGES, FREIGHT, &c.

ALSO, FOR THE COLLECTION OF NOTES, DRAFTS & ACCOUNTS IN ALL THE CITIES, TOWNS & VILLAGES IN THE EASTERN, WESTERN, SOUTHERN & SOUTH-WESTERN STATE

his family.

Carnegie also invested in the Woodruff Sleeping Car Company, which made sleeping cars for trains. He knew that as more and more people relied on train travel, sleeping cars would be vital to the growth of the Pennsylvania Railroad and other railway lines. This, too, turned out to be a successful investment that brought him lots of money.

> *Railroads were vital to the growth of America. When Carnegie worked for the railroad, it ended at the Mississippi River. In the 1860s, efforts toward the first transcontinental railroad began. Tracks from the west and east met in Utah in 1869. People could now travel across the entire country by rail.*

In 1856, Scott was promoted to be the general superintendent of the Pennsylvania Railroad in Altoona. Of course, he wanted Andrew to come with him. Carnegie moved his family to a nice house there, and even insisted on hiring a servant for his mother. She resisted, but since he was making more money, he wanted to make her life a little easier.

Then Scott was made vice president of the Pennsylvania Railroad. He moved to Philadelphia, but Carnegie did not go with him. They parted ways. Carnegie later wrote:

> *[Scott] was one of the most delightful superiors that anyone could have and I soon became warmly attached to him. He*

*was my great man and all the hero wor-
ship that is inherent in youth I showered
upon him.*

Even though he was losing his mentor, all was
not lost for Andrew. In fact, Scott appointed
Carnegie the new superintendent of the Pittsburgh
division of the Pennsylvania Railroad, the same
job Scott held when Carnegie began working for
him. So in 1859, Carnegie moved his family back to
Pittsburgh. Carnegie was thrilled with the
position and claimed he would do it even if he
wasn't getting paid. He was, however, given a nice
salary. He made his brother Tom a telegraph operator. Carnegie also became the first man to hire
female telegraphers.

As Pittsburgh became a booming center of
industry, it grew dirty and sooty from the smoke-
stacks of its many factories. Used to the quiet, clean
environment that they enjoyed in Altoona, Carnegie
bought a house in Homewood Estates, a suburb outside the city. Their new home had a lovely garden for
his mother. There, they met and socialized with
people of educated and refined backgrounds.

At the age of 24, Carnegie had risen to an important role in the railroad industry. He had not reached
his peak, yet, and was always looking for ways to
grow. "I was pleased every day," he wrote, "to feel
that I was learning something new." ❧

6 DIVIDED BY WAR, UNITED BY RAILROADS

Chapter

ოოო

Carnegie's strong will and work ethic were soon needed by his country. In April 1861, the Civil War broke out between the Northern and Southern states. The Southern states wanted to secede from the North, to protect, among other things, their right to hold slaves. President Abraham Lincoln wanted to keep the country together and end slavery.

Carnegie's former employer, Thomas Scott, was appointed assistant secretary of war in charge of transportation and communication. He immediately called on Carnegie to come to Washington, D.C., to assist him. He trusted Carnegie's knowledge of telegraph and railroad lines. Both would be needed in the war effort—telegraph lines for relaying information through the North and railroads to

The Battle of Bull Run, one of the first battles of the Civil War, showed the Union Army that the South would not be easily defeated.

transport the troops and supplies.

At this time in history, most railroads were in the North and few in the South. The line leading into Washington, the capital of the United States, was especially important.

Southern soldiers had tried to cut off this line of communication between Washington and the North by ripping up track and cutting down telegraph lines. The North desperately needed these lines to be in place. They carried troops to their destinations, and then carried supplies to the troops once they were in place. Also, if there was no communication from Washington with the North, the South could easily invade the city and take President Lincoln captive.

Upon his arrival in Washington, Carnegie's first job was to get the track into the city up and running. Carnegie gathered a crew of track, bridge, and road builders. In only three days, with little sleep and constant work, Carnegie and his men got this lifeline working again.

Riding the engine on the way back to Washington to test the railway, Carnegie noticed one of the telegraph lines was down. In fact, the line was pinned to the ground with a stake. He ordered the train to stop so he could free the line. When he did, however, the line struck him across the cheek, cutting a large gash. Even though he wasn't in battle,

Carnegie's scar always reminded him of his work during the war.

The Union Army used railroads to transport troops and supplies.

Besides fixing the lines, Carnegie also needed to run telegraph operations. He worked in nearby Alexandria, Virginia, training telegraph operators. They were to send important messages about movement of troops and needed supplies. Then news came over the wire. The Battle of Bull Run, one of the first of the war, broke out on July 21. As many trains as could be spared needed to rush to the front to get the men out of there. The North was being defeated and retreating at a furious pace. The telegraph office was only a few miles from the front. But Carnegie's telegraph operators stayed at their posts and kept the lines of communication open even as soldiers rushed by them in confused mobs.

Carnegie rode on the trains, loaded men onto stretchers, and brought back wounded soldiers. They made numerous trips. Carnegie was dismayed by all the death and injury war had caused.

His next post was in the War Building in Washington, D.C., working alongside Scott. He came in contact with President Lincoln almost daily. Carnegie greatly admired the president. Lincoln would come into the telegraph office and sit at Carnegie's desk to find out the latest news. Carnegie was most impressed with the way the president treated everyone he met as an equal. "I never met a great man who so thoroughly made himself one with all men as Mr. Lincoln," Carnegie wrote. The war lasted until 1865,

Carnegie had worked—and been successful—in a number of different fields before he was 30 years old.

but Carnegie did not stay in Washington. He returned to Pittsburgh in November 1861. He had trained his men well and felt confident leaving the important telegraph work to them. His railway in Pittsburgh was busier than ever, transporting thousands of troops. He needed to go home.

Carnegie always kept watch for a good business opportunity, wanting to grow with America. He was already involved in the railroad business, but he wanted to find some other profitable investments as well. Carnegie asked himself what he could invest in that was needed by the railroad industry. Iron was the answer.

President Abraham Lincoln was assassinated less than a week after the end of the Civil War.

Pittsburgh was the place to be. Many factories in Pittsburgh were already making iron. Railroad tracks and locomotives were both made of iron. Railroads were becoming a vital part of the United States and a new source of freedom. During the Civil War, the railroads crossing the countryside moved men and supplies from battle to battle and camp to camp. After the war, people wanted to move more freely around the nation. There were cities to visit and work to be found in them. There were lands to settle in the West. As new towns were established, railroads were built to join them. Railroads were helping to unite the nation. And as the country grew, it would need thousands of miles of tracks, as well as locomotives to run on them.

Carnegie wanted to find an iron product that no one had thought of before. John Piper, whom Carnegie knew from his Altoona days, gave Carnegie an idea. Pipe, as Carnegie called him, had built a model of a bridge made of iron and was looking for investors. Until then, bridges were made of wood. But the smallest of sparks from a train could set them on fire. Flooding rivers toppled bridges with their torrents of water. Wooden bridges had long been a problem that delayed trains for days until they could be rebuilt.

Iron bridges, Carnegie thought, would be much more reliable. With the United States growing and new railroads being built everyday, there would be many rivers to cross. Carnegie, Piper, and a group of other men formed a partnership in 1863, which became known as the Keystone Bridge Company. They opened several workshops throughout Pittsburgh. In Pittsburgh, where the tracks of many railroads met in the city, they were in a perfect position to secure contracts for building bridges

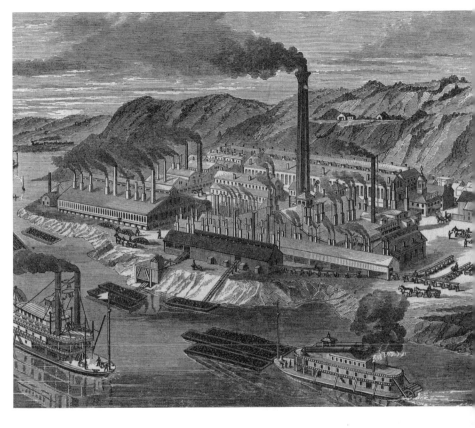

Pittsburgh's American Iron Works Factory was a major U.S. iron producer.

from countless customers. The company was an immediate success.

The Keystone Bridge Company name was stamped on the sides of many bridges built in the United States. When there were large and formidable rivers to cross, such as the 300 feet (91 meters) of the Ohio River, or the more than 500 feet (152 m) of the Mississippi, some people didn't think it could be done. But Carnegie proved them wrong. Iron was definitely the superior material for building bridges, and all the railroads needed them.

"The surest foundation of a manufacturing concern is quality," Carnegie wrote. "After that, and a long way after, comes cost." He took pride in how well the bridges were built. As his company grew, he experimented with new methods of manufacturing iron. Wrought iron, he soon found, was stronger than cast iron. He would only build "a safe structure or none at all." Customers grew to trust him and his bridges.

This railroad bridge was built by the Keystone Bridge Company.

In 1865, the year the Civil War ended, Carnegie decided to retire from his job at the Pennsylvania Railroad. He wanted to devote his time to his investment in the iron business. Never again would he be paid a salary. He would make money the rest of his life through his investments and running his own businesses.

Besides the Keystone Bridge Company, Carnegie had also invested in oil. He had bought a farm with a seemingly unending supply of oil under it that earned lots of money for him. He also looked for business opportunities with other industries connected to the railroad. His investment in sleeping cars continued to pay off. He also founded companies that made locomotives and rails, and he sold bonds to other investors to raise money for railroads.

Before plunging into new business ventures, however, Carnegie intended to enjoy himself. He and two friends spent nine months traveling through Europe, visiting museums, seeing plays, and listening to concerts. They also enjoyed spending time outdoors. In late 1866, Carnegie returned to

There are a few types of iron. Wrought iron is nearly pure iron. In its hard form, it can be hammered or bent into the shape needed. Cast iron, a less pure form of iron, cannot be made into shapes by hammering. It must be melted until it is liquid and then poured into molds. Pig iron is the least pure form of iron; it is the iron most often used to make steel.

Pittsburgh ready to embark on a new stage of his business life.

When Carnegie's younger brother Tom married a woman named Lucy Coleman in 1867, Carnegie decided to let them live in the house at Homewood Estates. He had his eyes set on New York City, where many big investors conducted their business. He would be closer to the banks and be more able to manage his growing wealth.

Carnegie and his mother moved to the big city in the East. New York City opened up a new financial world for Carnegie. In the mid-1800s, New York City was becoming the financial capital of the United States, and Carnegie opened up his office near Wall Street, the financial center of New York City. The city also introduced Carnegie to a new social world as well. He and his mother lived in very luxurious surroundings—first at the St. Nicholas Hotel and then the Windsor Hotel—in their own private suites. Carnegie was eager to tap into the cultural opportunities New York offered. He joined the elite Nineteenth Century Club, an exclusive group that met to discuss and hear lectures about

One reason Carnegie's investments were so successful is because he had personal experience with the industries in which he invested. Having worked in a telegraph office, for the railroads, and in iron mills, Carnegie had an insider's understanding that helped him make sound investment decisions.

various topics of the day. He also loved to roam the large museums and art galleries in New York and listen to concerts in the music halls. ❧

Carnegie and his mother made their home in New York City's luxurious Windsor Hotel.

63 ☙

7 KING STEEL

⁓⊱⧓⊰⁓

With Carnegie in the lead, iron became the most common building material for bridges. There was a problem with iron, however. It often had to be replaced. Even the strongest iron rails were replaced every few months or less.

Another building material, steel, could last for years. While iron is a metal that is found in nature, steel had to be man-made by heating iron until it was molten, or liquid. Some elements, such as carbon, were burned out of it. What was left was a stronger, sturdier building material that could be molded into shapes.

Not many companies invested in steel because it cost too much to make. It took large equipment and a lot of time. Steel was used to make small items, such as knives, needles, and scissors. Large items of steel, however, would be much too expensive. A man in England, Henry Bessemer, however, had discovered a way to make steel easily and cheaply. He developed a method in 1856 that became known as the Bessemer process.

Carnegie had heard of the Bessemer process, but had not been convinced steel would be a good investment, especially since iron seemed to be a strong enough material for use on the railroads. In 1872, however, he changed his mind. That year, during a tour of Europe, Carnegie was able to meet Bessemer in England and witness production at a steel mill.

The Bessemer converter was a tall egg-shaped furnace, about 12 feet (3.6 meters) high, that could be turned onto its side by a large wheel. The furnace was an open container filled with liquid iron. Blasts of cold air shot into the container to burn off the carbon. Huge jets of white flame rose out of the converter with a deafening roar. The container was wheeled onto its side and the molten steel poured out into molds.

Henry Bessemer (1813–1898) of Britain learned about working with metals from his father. He developed a one-step process of making steel that was 10 times faster than what had been done before. His timing was perfect. Railroads needed steel, and he had the best method for making it.

Steelworkers used many different tools to create steel products.

Carnegie was impressed with the new converter, and he was ready to invest. Steel could finally be produced in a way that made it affordable. As he had predicted with iron, Carnegie knew America would definitely have uses for steel. Rails, locomotives, and bridges would all need to be strong to accommodate the growing traffic as more people expanded settlements to the west.

His partners in the iron business were not willing to switch over to steel so quickly. So he sought out new investors. Soon, he found the perfect location for a steel mill outside of Pittsburgh. It was near the Ohio River, which allowed for easy transport of goods by water. It was also near the lines of both the Pennsylvania and the Baltimore and Ohio railroads. Not only would these two railroads be needing his services, but they would allow his steel to reach all areas of the United States.

It was a difficult time to take on a new building venture. In 1873, the United States was suffering from an economic depression. Many factories and businesses ran out of money. They closed and left thousands of people out of work. Unlike many other wealthy men of his time, Carnegie had saved a lot of money. Instead of needing a loan for such a large building venture, then, Carnegie had his own money to spend. Labor was cheap. With so many people looking for jobs, it was easy to find skilled laborers to build his mill and train on the new equipment.

Carnegie's Edgar Thomson Steel Works received its first contract for steel rails in 1875. Once it began production, it was instantly successful. Soon, the Edgar Thomson Steel Works was just one of many

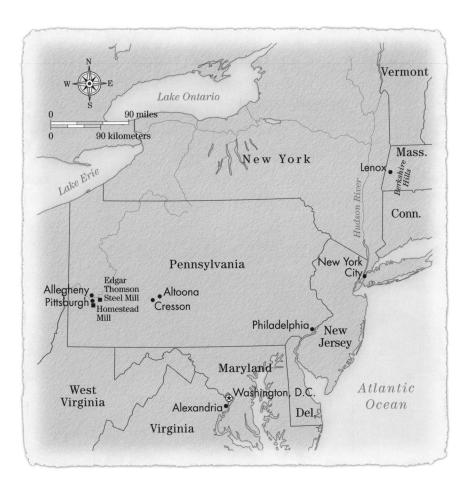

mills in the Carnegie Steel Company. As Carnegie's company grew, he looked for ways to improve business. He hired chemists to make sure the science behind the process was up-to-date. He refined an open-hearth method of making steel, which lowered the cost of steel even more. He bought iron mines so he would always have the materials needed to make the steel.

Many of the places Carnegie was associated with during his lifetime were in the vicinity of Pittsburgh, Pennsylvania.

The uses for steel grew as well. Steel was used to make farm and factory machines. It formed the hulls of ships. It was molded into girders to hold up skyscrapers and the elevators inside them. Steel was also used for subway lines and for water and gas pipes underground.

Carnegie Steel became the main producer of steel in the United States, and America in turn dominated steel production worldwide. "Farewell, then,

Carnegie's efforts enabled the United States to dominate the steel industry.

A STEEL CINCH ON THE WORLD

Age of Iron; all hail, King Steel," he declared. Because he controlled this dominant industry, Carnegie became known as a "captain of industry." Money poured in, and his wealth grew daily. Managing his money became a full-time job. Even though he worked hard, however, he still made time to travel. Scotland became his favorite place to visit, where he kept in constant communication with his many companies by cablegrams.

> *Carnegie's mills provided building materials for many important 19th-century buildings. The first skyscraper in the United States, Chicago's Home Insurance Company building, was built with iron and steel from Carnegie's Homestead Works. The 50-story-high Washington Monument, however, was Carnegie's proudest building achievement.*

Carnegie also liked to visit his mills in Pittsburgh. In 1880, he bought a small home in Cresson, outside of Pittsburgh, where he and his mother could escape the heat of New York during the summer.

Carnegie's mother had been feeling ill, so in 1886, he brought her to Cresson to rest. Then Carnegie caught typhoid and became sick as well. Their luck worsened when Carnegie's brother Tom was suddenly struck with pneumonia. While Carnegie lay sick in his bed, both his mother and brother died within days of each other. Carnegie was devastated. He felt he was alone in the world.

Carnegie had lived with his mother his entire

life. Now, returning to New York, he faced an empty house. He had never married, mostly because his mother did not want him to. She had never felt any woman was good enough for him. Carnegie always supported her and cared for her, and she had enjoyed that attention. Now that his mother was gone, however, Carnegie now felt he could marry.

Carnegie had a woman in mind. He had been courting Louise Whitfield in New York since the early 1880s. The pair had met through Louise's father, a wealthy New York merchant with whom Carnegie did business. They had often ridden horses together in Central Park. She was more than 20 years younger than he—Carnegie was 51 and Whitfield was 29. At one point, they had even been secretly engaged.

Carnegie had the opportunity to meet many women, but Louise truly took his heart. He wrote, "In the end the others all faded into ordinary beings. Miss Whitfield remained alone as the perfect one beyond any I had met." On April 22, 1887, Carnegie and Louise married. His wedding present to her was a house on West 51st Street in New York City, which they shared together.

The Carnegies' first trip together as a married couple was to Dunfermline. He was eager to introduce her to his Uncle Lauder and other relatives and friends. Louise enjoyed her time in Scotland, and

soon they were spending so much time in Carnegie's native land that he was criticized for disloyalty to his adopted country. A British friend went so far as to call him "the star-spangled Scotchman."

Carnegie waited until after his mother died to marry Louise Whitfield.

8

TROUBLE AND RETIREMENT

ೞ⭗ಌ

Andrew Carnegie's life was full. He was happily married and had truly become the captain of his industry. He did his best to hire good men below him to manage his businesses and thousands of laborers. In a vast empire, however, with so many employees, there were bound to be some problems.

Carnegie valued his laborers and respected their skills in his mills. But their working conditions were not ideal. They worked 12 hours a day every day in a bleak and dangerous environment where men sometimes suffered ghastly injuries. Unions formed to protect workers from unfair conditions and to ensure the workers were being paid and treated fairly.

Carnegie's workers were paid on a sliding scale.

Armed guards from the Pinkerton Detective Agency were hired to protect Carnegie's mill during the Homestead Riot.

When the company was making profits, the workers did well. But when business was bad, wages went down. The laborers did not believe this was fair, yet Carnegie held firm. He kept wages low so that he could keep the cost of steel low as well. Some of Carnegie's workers had gone on strike demanding higher wages. Carnegie closed the plant instead of giving in. But he did promise the men their jobs when they decided to meet his terms. He respected their right to disagree with him, yet he was not willing to pay them any more.

In the summer of 1892, with the mills running smoothly, Carnegie left for an extended vacation in Scotland. Henry Clay Frick, the executive head of the Carnegie Steel Company, was left in charge of the Homestead Mill, one of Carnegie's mills near Pittsburgh. Soon, however, trouble began.

The Homestead workers who belonged to a union were demanding more pay. But Carnegie and Frick refused. If anything, they wanted to cut wages because the mill's contract with the union had expired.

Frick closed the mills and locked them up until the workers agreed to the new terms. Frick was afraid the workers might try to storm the mill. He ordered that a high fence strung with barbed wire be built around the entire grounds. He also hired 300 armed guards from the Pinkerton Detective Agency.

They would protect the mill in case of a riot.

Frick was right. The workers were mad. Soon they blocked the roads to the mill. An angry mob formed outside the walls. Because the roads were blocked, the Pinkerton guards arrived on barges on the river. As the barges pulled near the dock to

A weekly paper covered the growing violence at the Homestead Mill.

the Homestead Mill, someone from the mob fired at the guards. Shots filled the sky between the guards and the workmen. The fight lasted for hours.

It was a loud, violent, and chaotic evening. Several workers and Pinkerton guards were killed. The government finally sent in troops to calm the mob and chaos that had developed in town.

Carnegie was sure that if he had been there, the situation would not have grown to such a dangerous scale. He would have handled things differently. While Frick was always harsh with the workers, Carnegie valued their skill. When he received news of the strike, however, Carnegie did not come right home. Frick had asked him not to, but the public still blamed Carnegie for the horrible incident.

The mills were closed for months while the situation was being resolved. When Carnegie did come back to Pittsburgh, he addressed the workers and their wives, expressing his sorrow for the situation. He compared the company's success to a three-legged stool. The money needed to run it, the laborers who did the work, and the management who ran the company were equally important in keeping it up and running.

Carnegie had spent his life on a quest for success and certainly attained his goal. Now his life slowly started to focus on other things besides work. On March 30, 1897, Carnegie and his wife Louise welcomed the birth of a baby girl, whom they named after Carnegie's mother, Margaret.

Carnegie also bought land in Scotland so he could spend time in both countries he loved. In 1898, he purchased an ancient castle that was practically in ruins, but it was on beautiful land. Carnegie completely renovated the buildings and grounds and called his new estate Skibo. This new home was made of pinkish colored stone and was complete with towers and turrets. He and his family spent much time there, swimming in its pool or tending to

Skibo is located on 7,500 acres (3,000 hectares) of parkland in the Scottish highlands.

the gardens. He held grand gatherings, often inviting famous people of the day, but he also enjoyed more quiet moments to fish, golf, or sit and write.

The Carnegie Steel Company was the controlling force in the steel industry. It produced products as varied as large steel girders and tiny carpenter nails. As the United States entered a new century, Carnegie was ready to sell his business and retire. But there was a problem. Carnegie Steel was worth so much money that there were not many people who could afford to buy it.

J.P. Morgan (1837–1913) enjoyed rich living and spent much of his fortune on his art collections. After his death, some works from his collections went to the Metropolitan Museum of Art in New York City, which he had helped found. Morgan also was a famous yachtsman who financed several winners of the America's Cup yacht race.

One man with enough money, however, was John Pierpont Morgan. He was one of the most powerful men in the United States. Morgan was a banker who excelled in forming large corporations. He had created the largest private bank in the United States and was trying to control the steel industry as well. Carnegie Steel was a competitor, and Morgan needed Carnegie's company in order to succeed. The price tag was high. Carnegie offered to sell it for $480 million. Morgan eagerly paid.

The Carnegie Steel Company

continued with a new owner
and a new name—it was
now part of the U.S. Steel
Corporation. The addi-
tion of Carnegie Steel
made U.S. Steel the
largest corporation
in the world at the
time, and the sale of
his company made
Andrew Carnegie the
richest man in the United
States. Carnegie was ready
to escape business life and
retire a wealthy man. ℥

*John Pierpont
Morgan*

9 THE RESPONSIBILITY OF FORTUNE

‿୧◡◠୨‿

At age 66, after years of work, Andrew Carnegie saw his retirement as a chance to fulfill what he felt was the responsibility of a man with such a fortune. He must find ways to give his money away.

He was not opposed to wealth. After all, he had spent the majority of his life trying to attain it. But his wealth did not just belong to him. It was nobler, he believed, that "man should labor, not for himself alone, but in and for a brotherhood of his fellows." He did not want to leave his fortune to his family—he felt it would be a burden for his wife and daughter to have to handle so much money. He also did not want to have to wait until his death before his money was given to helpful causes.

In the late 1800s and early 1900s, Carnegie

Andrew Carnegie felt a responsibility to share the wealth he had earned.

published numerous books on the subject of distributing wealth and the responsibility of millionaires like himself. Even though he earned his money through his own skills and good choices, he did not believe it was his to keep. The responsibility of attaining such a large fortune included giving it back to mankind. He believed the life of a rich man had two stages—making the money and then giving it away. So in the early 1900s, Carnegie "resolved to stop accumulating and begin the infinitely more serious task of wise distribution."

Carnegie became one of the leading philanthropists of his day. Giving away his money occupied all his time. Remembering Colonel Anderson, the man from his youth who had shared his personal library with working boys, Carnegie focused his attention on libraries. Even before his retirement, he donated funds for a library in his hometown of Dunfermline, Scotland, in 1881. In 1890, Carnegie gave a library, as well as a music and lecture hall, to the city of Allegheny, Pennsylvania, where he had grown up in the United States. He gave New York City numerous libraries and Carnegie Hall to host magnificent concerts by world-famous musicians.

Pittsburgh, the city that grew as his success did, received the Carnegie Institute of Pittsburgh in 1907 (now Carnegie-Mellon University). In a speech Carnegie gave at the dedication, he expressed his

New York City's Carnegie Hall hosts some of the world's great performances.

own wonder at what his money could do. He said he felt like Aladdin

when he saw this building and was aware that he had put it up, but he could not bring himself to a consciousness of having done it any more than if he had produced the same effect by rubbing a lamp.

Soon, giving away free libraries became a

Carnegie wrote in his autobiography, "It was from my own early experience that I decided there was no use to which money could be applied so productive of good to boys and girls who have good within them and ability and ambition to develop it, as the founding of a public library in a community which is willing to support it as a municipal institution."

business. Carnegie hired secretaries to shuffle through all the requests and applications. Carnegie donated the funds to build the library building, and the community was in charge of providing the land, filling the library with books, and keeping the library going into the future. Some people criticized him for this. After all, if the community needed a library, why couldn't he pay for the books, too? He could certainly afford it. But Carnegie believed that a library should be a community responsibility. If a town truly wanted one, they should be willing to invest in it themselves as well.

In all, Carnegie gave 2,811 libraries to communities in the United States and throughout the world as far away as New Zealand and the Fiji Islands. On many, Carnegie asked that over their entrances, the words "Let There Be Light" be carved with the image of a rising sun to represent the knowledge that would be found within.

Another gift Carnegie often gave to communities was a church organ. He first gave an organ to the church his father attended before he died. When

others heard about the gift, requests began to pour in. He gave about 5,000 organs to churches in the United States and almost 3,000 more organs to churches around the world.

Carnegie donated a library to the city of Stillwater, Minnesota.

Carnegie also wanted to support those who had helped him throughout his life. One group was his workers. He set up the Andrew Carnegie Relief Fund to help laborers and their families. He sought out old friends and kept a private list of people on his pension list. He made sure these friends and their families would not have to worry about money for the rest of their lives. He set up the Railroad

Pension Fund to have funds available for the "old boys" of the Pittsburgh Division where he had worked. "It is indeed, more blessed to give than to receive," he said. "These dear good friends would do for me and mine as I do for them were positions reversed. I am sure of this." He also set up a Hero's Fund to help the families of those who died helping or saving others.

Although he only went to school for a short time in his youth, Carnegie felt it was important to fund education. He established the Carnegie Institution in Washington, D.C., in 1902. This foundation was devoted to science and the pursuit of knowledge. Carnegie was especially interested in astronomy, and money from the Carnegie Institution also went to create the Mount Wilson Observatory in California, where a huge telescope searched the skies for new discoveries.

Some of the Carnegie Institution's leading researchers from the early and middle years of the 20th century are well-known. They include aviator Charles Lindbergh, who made aerial surveys of archaeological sites, Edwin Hubble, who discovered that the universe is expanding and that there are galaxies other than our own, and Charles Richter, who created the earthquake measurement scale.

He founded the Carnegie Foundation for the Advancement of Teaching in 1905, which gave money to professors in their retirement. He supported smaller

Carnegie donated the Mount Wilson Observatory, including its large telescope, the Hooke Reflector.

colleges that needed funds to grow, especially those that educated children of the working class. He also gave money to help struggling black colleges, such as the Hampton and Tuskegee institutes, so that

Carnegie (second from right) and other American leaders celebrated the 25th anniversary of Tuskegee Institute with its founder, Booker T. Washington (center).

everyone in the United States would have an open door to education.

Carnegie also returned to his roots. He could never forget the beautiful abbey and palace that had meant so much to him as a child in Dunfermline. The area had been closed to visitors, but Carnegie was able to purchase all the land and make it into a public park. He wanted the hardworking people of the town, especially the children, to have a chance to enjoy the "sweetness and light" that he felt pervaded the ruins and beautiful glen surrounding them. On the grounds, areas for concerts and gatherings were built, as well as fields and pools for children to play in.

Even though Carnegie was giving away his millions, he was still making millions on his many investments. No matter how much he donated to worthy causes, he still had a fortune left, and it was growing. The task of distributing his money was too great for him.

In 1911, he created the Carnegie Corporation of New York. The corporation was in charge of distributing his wealth to those who needed it. He kept some out for his family and gave the rest of his fortune for the corporation to give away. In all, Carnegie gave away more than $350 million during his lifetime.

The images of wounded soldiers and bloody battlefields stayed with Carnegie since his

> *Carnegie wrote a number of books over the course of his lifetime, including* An American Four-in-Hand in Britain, Round the World, Triumphant Democracy, The Gospel of Wealth, The Empire of Business, The Life of James Watt, Problems of Today, *and* Autobiography of Andrew Carnegie.

experience with the Civil War. Carnegie became a pacifist and opposed war of all kinds. He wanted to do what he could to bring peace to the world.

In 1910, he established the Carnegie Endowment for International Peace. He tried to get nations together—Great Britain, the United States, Germany, Russia, and France—to promise they would never go to war. He became the president of the New York Peace Society and spread the word through articles and speeches. When threat of war surfaced, Carnegie met with world leaders and wrote to presidents.

At The Hague in the Netherlands, where nations met to talk about how to prevent war during peacetime, Carnegie built the Peace Palace. The building included an international law library as well as meeting places for nations to convene.

But even a man with millions of dollars soon found that money could not buy world peace. He did all he could to prevent war. Carnegie was both saddened and shocked when World War I broke out in 1914.

Carnegie was growing old. When the war began, Carnegie left Skibo and would never go back. Now in his 80s, he was struck with pneumonia. He recovered, but was never quite the same. To ensure rest and peace for himself, he bought a mansion in Massachusetts in the Berkshire Hills, called

Shadowbrook, in 1916.

Even though Carnegie was growing weak and fragile, he found happiness in the marriage of his daughter Margaret to Roswell Miller in April 1919. In

The Peace Palace is the home of the Court of International Justice.

Even in his old age, Carnegie enjoyed outdoor activities such as walking with his dog.

August, however, his health took a turn for the worse. During a restful visit to Shadowbrook, pneumonia struck again. Carnegie died peacefully in his sleep on the morning of August 11, 1919. He was 84 years old.

Carnegie was called the richest man in the world. From his first salary of $1.20 a week as a bobbin boy, he climbed up the ladder from poverty to fortune. Always excelling in every task he was given, Carnegie valued hard work as the key to success. His standards for himself and others were high. He craved prosperity, and for a man who stood just over 5 feet (150 centimeters) tall, he became a character larger than life—the captain of an industry he created in the United States.

Carnegie's attitude toward money was unmatched in his time and perhaps unmatched since. He did not believe in working for the individual's benefit. His money was for the community. And knowledge, he felt, was one of the best ways to serve people. By providing people with libraries, everyone—from the hardworking bobbin boy to the captain of industry—could have access to the light of knowledge and success.

CARNEGIE'S LIFE

1835

Born on November 25 in Dunfermline, Scotland

1848

Moves from Scotland to the United States; gets first job as a bobbin boy

1850

Works as a telegraph operator

1850

1840

Auguste Rodin, famous sculptor of *The Thinker*, is born

1850

Jeans are invented by Levi Strauss, a German who moved to California during the gold rush

WORLD EVENTS

1859

Becomes the superin-
tendent of the
Pittsburgh division of
the Pennsylvania
Railroad

1861

Works in Washington;
the American Civil
War begins

1853

Works for the
Pennsylvania Railroad
Company

1860

1858

English scientist
Charles Darwin
presents his theory
of evolution

CARNEGIE'S LIFE

1863

Forms an iron
bridge company, later
called the Keystone
Bridge Company

1865

Retires from
railroad work

1867

Leaves Pittsburgh
for New York

1865

1863

Thomas Nast draws the
modern Santa Claus for
Harper's Weekly, although
Santa existed previously

1865

Lewis Carrol writes
*Alice's Adventures in
Wonderland*

WORLD EVENTS

1875

Carnegie's Edgar Thomson Steel Mill begins production

1881

Donates first public library to his hometown of Dunfermline

1887

Marries Louise Whitfield on April 22

1880

1881

The first Japanese political parties are formed

1886

Grover Cleveland dedicates the Statue of Liberty in New York, a gift from the people of France

CARNEGIE'S LIFE

1892
Combines three companies to form Carnegie Steel Company; steelworkers at the Homestead Mill strike

1889
Publishes essay, "Wealth"

1897
Daughter Margaret is born

1890

1893
Women gain voting privileges in New Zealand, the first country to take such a step

WORLD EVENTS

1901

Sells the Carnegie Steel Company to J.P. Morgan

1910

Establishes the Carnegie Endowment for International Peace

1919

Dies on August 11 at Shadowbrook

1910

1901

Britain's Queen Victoria dies

1917

Vladimir Lenin and Leon Trotsky lead Bolsheviks in a rebellion against the czar of Russia during the October Revolution

DATE OF BIRTH: November 25, 1835

BIRTHPLACE: Dunfermline, Scotland

FATHER: William Carnegie

MOTHER: Margaret Morrison Carnegie

EDUCATION: Four years at the Rolland School in Scotland

SPOUSE: Louise Whitfield Carnegie (1857–1946)

DATE OF MARRIAGE: April 22, 1887

CHILDREN: Margaret Carnegie Miller (1897–1990)

DATE OF DEATH: August 11, 1919

PLACE OF BURIAL: Sleepy Hollow Cemetery, Tarrytown, New York

In the Library

Carnegie, Andrew. *Autobiography of Andrew Carnegie.* Boston: Houghton Mifflin, 1920.

Edge, Laura B. *Andrew Carnegie.* Minneapolis: Lerner Publications, 2004.

Kent, Zachary. *Andrew Carnegie: Steel King and Friend to Libraries.* Springfield, N.J.: Enslow Publishers, 1999.

Meltzer, Milton. *The Many Lives of Andrew Carnegie.* Danbury, Conn.: Franklin Watts, 1997.

Outman, James L., and Elisabeth M. Outman. *Industrial Revolution Biographies.* Detroit: Thomson Gale, 2003.

Look for more Signature Lives
books about this era:

Carrie Chapman Catt: *A Voice for Women*
Henry B. Gonzalez: *Congressman of the People*
J. Edgar Hoover: *Controversial FBI Director*
Langston Hughes: *The Voice of Harlem*
Douglas MacArthur: *America's General*
Eleanor Roosevelt: *First Lady of the World*
Elizabeth Cady Stanton: *Social Reformer*

On the Web

For more information on *Andrew Carnegie*, use FactHound to track down Web sites related to this book.

1. Go to *www.facthound*.com
2. Type in a search word related to this book or this book ID: 0756509955
3. Click on the *Fetch It* button.

FactHound will find the best Web sites for you.

Historic Sites

Carnegie Museum of Natural History
4400 Forbes Ave.
Pittsburgh, PA 15213
412/622-3131
To visit a museum donated to the city of Pittsburgh by Andrew Carnegie

Andrew Carnegie Birthplace
Moodie Street, Dunfermline
Fife, Scotland KY12 7PL
Tel: (+44) 0 1383 723638
To visit the site in Scotland where Carnegie was born

abbey
a church that is also home to monks or nuns

bobbin
a large spool of thread used by weavers

corporation
a business that has a legal identity separate from
that of its founder or owner

gallery
the upper seats in a theater

investing
putting money into a business in hopes it will
earn a profit

mentor
one who teaches someone else

molten
the hot, liquid form of metal

Morse code
a system of signaling using dots and dashes that
represent letters of the alphabet

pacifist
someone who strongly believes that war and
violence are wrong and refuses to fight

philanthropists
people who give away their wealth to help others

secede
to break away from

strike
when people refuse to work, hoping to force their
company to agree to their demands

Source Notes

Chapter 1

Page 10, line 25: Andrew Carnegie. *Our Coaching Trip: Brighton to Inverness.* New York: Private Circulation, 1882, p. 152. As quoted in Joseph Frazier Wall. *Andrew Carnegie.* Pittsburgh: University of Pittsburgh Press, 1989, p. 408.

Chapter 2

Page 15, line 8: Andrew Carnegie. *Autobiography of Andrew Carnegie.* Boston: Houghton Mifflin, 1920, p. 7.

Page 19, line 3: Ibid., p. 13.

Page 19, line 12: Ibid., p. 14.

Page 22, line 3: Ibid.

Page 23, line 4: Ibid., p. 25.

Chapter 3

Page 25, line 2: Ibid., p. 26.

Page 29, line 25: Ibid., p. 31.

Page 30, line 16: Ibid., p. 34.

Page 33, line 1: Ibid., p. 37.

Chapter 4

Page 36, line 8: Ibid., p. 39.

Page 40, line 26: Ibid., p. 45.

Chapter 5

Page 50, line 25: Ibid., p. 70.

Page 51, line 27: Ibid., p. 95.

Chapter 6

Page 56, line 22: Ibid., p. 101.

Page 60, line 2: Ibid., p. 123.

Page 60, line 8: Ibid., p. 122.

Chapter 7

Page 70, line 9: Andrew Carnegie. *New York Evening Post.* 12 January, 1901. As quoted in Joseph Frazier Wall. *Andrew Carnegie.* Pittsburgh: University of Pittsburgh Press, 1989, p. 307.

Page 72, line 19: Ibid., p. 213.

Page 73, line 4: John S. Bowman. *Andrew Carnegie: Steel Tycoon.* Englewood Cliffs, N.J.: Silver Burdett Press, 1989, p. 85.

Chapter 9

Page 83, line 8: Andrew Carnegie. "Wealth." *North American Review.* June 1889. As quoted in http://alpha.furman.edu~benson/docs/carnegie.htm

Page 84, line 9: "Wealth."

Page 85, line 3: "Obituary for Andrew Carnegie." *New York Times*, 12 April 1919. As quoted in http://www.nytimes.com/learning/general/onthisday/bday/1125.html

Page 86, sidebar: *Autobiography of Andrew Carnegie*, p. 47.

Page 87, line 12: Ibid., p. 280.

Page 88, line 3: Ibid., p. 280.

Bowman, John S. *Andrew Carnegie: Steel Tycoon.* Englewood Cliffs, N.J.: Silver Burdett Press, 1989.

Carnegie, Andrew. *Autobiography of Andrew Carnegie.* Boston: Houghton Mifflin Company, 1920.

Carnegie, Andrew. "Wealth." *North American Review.* June 1889. http://alpha.furman.edu/~benson/docs/carnegie.htm

Fidler, Kathleen. *The Man Who Gave Away Millions.* New York: Roy Publishers, 1956.

History of Andrew Carnegie and Carnegie Libraries. http://www.andrewcarnegie.cc/

Judson, Clara Ingram. *Andrew Carnegie.* Chicago: Follett Publishing Company, 1964.

"The Richest Man in the World: Andrew Carnegie." *The American Experience.* Prod. Austin Hoyt. PBS. http://www.pbs.org/wgbh/amex/carnegie/index.html

Shippen, Katherine. *Andrew Carnegie and the Age of Steel.* New York, Random House, 1958.

Tedlow, Richard S. *Giants of Enterprise: Seven Business Innovators and the Empires They Built.* New York: HarperBusiness, 2001.

Wall, Joseph Frazier. *Andrew Carnegie.* Pittsburgh: University of Pittsburgh Press, 1989.

Dana Meachen Rau is an author, editor, and illustrator of children's books. She has written more than 100 books for children, many of them nonfiction in subjects including astronomy, history, and geography, as well as numerous biographies.

Ms. Rau loves her local library, which she visits at least once a week, and agrees with Carnegie's view that libraries are a wonderful place to start on a road to success. She lives in Burlington, Connecticut, with her husband and two children.